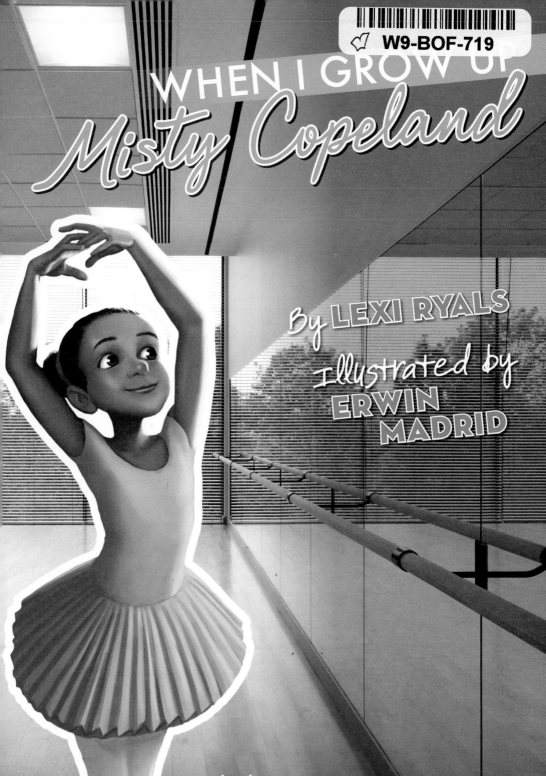

WHEN I GROW UP
Misty Copeland

By LEXI RYALS

Illustrated by
ERWIN MADRID

Scholastic Inc.

*Y*ou can do anything you want, even if you are being told negative things. Stay strong and find motivation.

— *Misty Copeland*

Photo Credits:

cover: WENN Ltd/Alamy Images; cover background: Arthur Kwiatkowski/iStockphoto; 1: Loop Images/ UIG via Getty Images; 3: Brian Kim Photography/Shutterstock, Inc.; 4: rusm/iStockphoto; 5: Jupiterimages/ Thinkstock; 6: Maxiphoto/iStockphoto; 6 inset: AP Images; 8-9: Ronnie Kaufman/Larry Hirshowitz/Getty Images; 10: LuckyImages/Fotolia; 11 left, 11 center: master1305/iStockphoto; 11 right: AYakovlev/iStockphoto; 12: Kevin Karzin/AP Images; 13: Shahrokh Rohani/iStockphoto; 13 inset left, 13 inset right: Natacha Pisarenko/ AP Images; 15: photoquest7/iStockphoto; 15 inset left: Acey Harper/The LIFE Images Collection/Getty Images; 15 inset right: Tongman501236/iStockphoto; 16: wdstock/iStockphoto; 17: Evgenyatamanenko/Dreamstime; 18: Littleny/Dreamstime; 20: Katherine Frey/The Washington Post via Getty Images; 21 left: ronniechua/ iStockphoto; 21 top right: Teradat Santivivut/iStockphoto; 21 bottom right: pidjoe/iStockphoto; 22-23: Andrea Mohin/The New York Times/Redux; 24: Warner Brothers/Everett Collection; 25: Andriy Bezuglov/Dreamstime; 26: Courtesy of Nik Apostolides; 27: Julieta Cervantes/The New York Times/Redux; 28 book: Chester Higgins Jr./The New York Times/Redux; 28 HDTV: Godfried Edelman/iStockphoto; 28 Misty at barre: Under Armour/AP Images; 28 tablet: GetWhatYSee/iStockphoto; 28 Misty on piano: Kevin Mazur/Getty Images; 29: focusstock/ Getty Images; 30: Carolyn Cole/Los Angeles Times/Contour by Getty Images; 31: FDAphoto/iStockphoto

This unauthorized biography was carefully researched to make sure it's accurate. Although the book is written to sound like Misty Copeland is speaking to the reader, these are not her actual statements.

Library of Congress Cataloging-in-Publication Data
Ryals, Lexi, author. When I grow up : Misty Copeland / by Lexi Ryals ; illustrations by Erwin Madrid.
New York, NY : Scholastic Nonfiction, 2016. | Series: Scholastic reader, level 3

ISBN 9781338032222 (paperback)

LCSH: Copeland, Misty | Ballet dancers—United States—Biography. | African American dancers—Biography.
BISAC: JUVENILE NONFICTION / Biography & Autobiography / Performing Arts.
JUVENILE NONFICTION / Biography & Autobiography / Women.
JUVENILE NONFICTION / Readers / Beginner.
GV1785.C635 R93 2016 792.8092 [B]—dc23 LC 2016013251

10 9 8 7 6 5 4 3 2 1   16 17 18 19 20

Printed in the U.S.A   40

First printing, September 2016

Book design by Marissa Asuncion

GLOSSARY

AUTOBIOGRAPHY: a biography written by the person it is about

BARRE: the horizontal wooden handrail in a ballet classroom that the dancer holds for support

CHOREOGRAPHING: the art of arranging and creating dances

CONVENT: a set of buildings occupied by nuns

CORPS DE BALLET: the chorus members in a ballet company

DRILL TEAM: a dance group that performs precise movements alongside a marching band

EN POINTE: dancing ballet wearing pointe shoes, which forces the ballerina to dance on the tips of her toes

HONE: to improve or perfect

LEOTARD: a tight one-piece garment worn especially by dancers, gymnasts, and acrobats

PAS DE DEUX: a ballet duet danced by a male and female dancer

POINTE SHOES: satin slippers with wooden blocks in the toes that allow ballerinas to dance on the tips of their toes

REHEARSAL: a practice session before a public appearance

SCHOLARSHIP: money given to a student to help pay for further education

UNDERSTUDY: a dancer who has studied another dancer's part in order to be his or her substitute in an emergency

TIME LINE

1982:
I was born on September 10, in Kansas City, Missouri.

1995:
I attended my first ballet class at the Boys & Girls Club of America.

1998:
I attended the San Francisco Ballet summer workshop.

1999:
I attended the American Ballet Theatre summer workshop.

2000:
I graduated from high school, attended my second ABT summer workshop, and joined the ABT Studio Company.

2001:
I was promoted to the ABT *corps de ballet*.

2007:
I was promoted to soloist in the ABT.

2012:
I danced the lead role in *The Firebird*.

2014:
My autobiography, *Life in Motion*, and my picture book, *Firebird*, were published.

2015:
I became the first African American woman to ever be named a principal dancer with the ABT, and I danced the dual lead in *Swan Lake*. I also made my Broadway debut in the musical *On the Town*.

My name is Misty Copeland. I was born on September 10, 1982, in Kansas City, Missouri. I grew up in San Pedro, California, with my mother and my older sister, Erica; older brothers, Chris and Doug; younger sister, Lindsey; and younger brother, Cameron.

We moved around a lot when I was growing up. Sometimes we lived in nice, big houses, and other times we lived in little apartments or motel rooms. Sometimes we had plenty of food, clothes, and toys, and other times we barely had enough to eat. Luckily, with five siblings, we always managed to have fun. I'm very close to my brothers and sisters, and we've always taken good care of one another.

So what's next for me? My job as a principal dancer will keep me pretty busy with classes, rehearsals, and performances, but I plan to keep learning, too! I want to dance the lead roles in all of the most famous classical ballets. It's important for dancers of all backgrounds to see a black woman in those roles. I want to continue introducing more people to ballet—especially people who look like me. I may not always be able to dance professionally, but I will never stop dancing!

I live in New York City, but I travel back home to California as often as I can to spend time with my family. When I'm not busy dancing, I love exploring "The Big Apple," seeing Broadway shows, visiting museums, and going out to eat—especially at seafood restaurants! I am so happy living out my dreams as a world-class professional ballerina.

Being in the ballet spotlight has given me other opportunities, too. I've done several major commercials and appeared on the cover of magazines like *Time*. I danced in a music video for Prince and performed with him at several of his concerts. I've also written two books: *Life in Motion*, which is my **autobiography**, and *Firebird*, which is a picture book for kids. Together with the Boys & Girls Clubs of America, I created an organization called Project Plié to help kids from all backgrounds discover ballet.

*I*n the spring of 2015, I danced the lead roles of Odette/Odile in *Swan Lake*. I was the first African American to ever do so on the Met stage. Then, in June, I was promoted to principal dancer. I couldn't have been happier or more proud of myself. I had worked so hard for so long. I had finally achieved my goal of becoming the first ever African American female principal dancer with ABT. Being a principal dancer means that everyone in the ballet world knows my name, and I get to dance the very best parts in each ballet. It is an honor and a dream come true.

In 2011, ABT announced that it would perform a ballet called *The Firebird*. The role of the Firebird was a very big part with two solos and a *pas de deux*. I was one of several ballerinas chosen to learn the part! I thought I would likely be an **understudy** since I had only been a soloist for four years. I was shocked when I was one of three ballerinas chosen to play the Firebird! It was the biggest role I'd ever been given. I practiced so hard that I injured my shin, but I didn't let that stop me from debuting as the Firebird on the Met stage. It got a lot of attention because it was one of the first times an African American ballerina

danced such a prominent role. It felt great to know that I was breaking boundaries and inspiring other dancers who looked different. It is still one of my favorite performances.

I spent six years dancing in the *corps de ballet*. During that time, I matured from a teenage dancer, who was a little unsure of herself, into a strong, capable woman who knew she deserved the spotlight. It is a challenge to be an African American ballerina because white dancers have always dominated ballet. I also stood out because, as I matured, my body shape changed. I had curves and no longer looked like the average ballet dancer. I had to turn my differences into strengths to achieve my goals. When I was promoted to a soloist spot, I felt honored, but I also knew that I had earned it. I was the first black soloist at ABT in over twenty years! Being a soloist meant that I got the chance to dance bigger and better parts.

*A*BT dancers work almost year-round, six days a week. In the fall, we perform at Lincoln Center. At Christmas, we often perform *The Nutcracker* at the Brooklyn Academy of Music. And in the spring, we perform at the Metropolitan Opera House. We start each day by warming up our muscles. Then we generally rehearse from noon until seven with a short lunch break. During performance weeks, we rehearse from 10:30 a.m. to 11:00 p.m.! We have about two months off in the summer. I keep myself busy with ballet classes, training, and other dance performances.

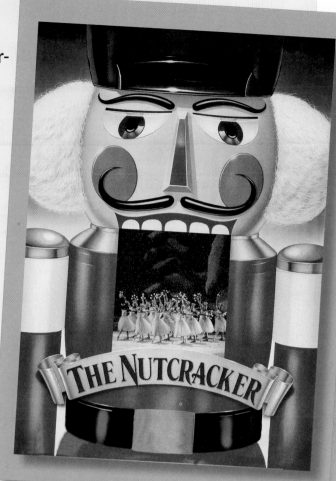

A ballet company is made up of soloists and principals who dance the main roles, as well as the *corps*. The *corps* is about fifty ballerinas who serve as the chorus. Dancers in the *corps* can be very competitive because each ballerina wants to be promoted to a soloist or principal dancer. During my first season in the *corps*, I had been chosen to dance the part of Clara in *The Nutcracker* that Christmas. It was a huge honor! But that season, I fractured my lower back. I had to sit out most of that year while I healed, so the role of Clara went to another ballerina.

When I returned to New York City, I started dancing for ABT's Studio Company. The Studio Company is made up of seven boys and seven girls who dance and train together for a year. If they do well in the Studio Company, they are asked to join the *corps* at the end of the year. The Studio Company traveled a lot, and I was able to dance some incredible roles including Aurora in the **pas de deux** from *Sleeping Beauty*. I loved being in the Studio Company, and it helped me grow more confident in my dancing before I joined the ABT *corps* when I was nineteen.

*B*efore I started in the Studio, I was invited to take a trip to China with ABT's **corps de ballet**. It was a big honor to be a guest dancer with the *corps* so early in my career. It gave me a taste of what I could look forward to someday. We performed in Shanghai, Taipei, and Singapore. I had just turned eighteen, and it was my first trip out of the country. It was an amazing experience to dance professionally with ABT and also get to sightsee and experience Chinese culture. It opened my eyes to how big the world was and how many places ballet could take me!

The next summer, I went back to ABT for a final summer workshop. I was done with high school, and I knew this could be the start of my professional ballet career. I'd been invited to live with Isabel Brown, one of the original ABT dancers. Isabel made sure I met lots of people who could help me in my dance career. I got the chance to dance the lead role in *Push Comes to Shove* for Twyla Tharp, a famous choreographer. Twyla's style is modern, edgy, and different from the classical ballet ABT is known for. Dancing for her proved to everyone that I could dance both modern and classical ballet. Things went so well that I accepted a spot in ABT's Studio Company!

Before I left, ABT awarded me the Coca-Cola Scholarship, which would pay for a year of supplies and training back in California. They also told me they would still have a spot for me next year. It meant a lot that the people at ABT believed in me and wanted me to dance for them. It was an extra honor because there weren't many African American ballerinas at the time. I went back home and enjoyed my senior year. I spent a lot of time dancing, but I also made time for normal high school stuff like sleepovers and prom.

With Diane's help, I **honed** my skills all year. That summer, I was accepted at ABT's summer workshop! Luckily, one of my best friends from the Lauridsen Ballet Center went, too. Most of the dancers roomed together at a **convent** in New York City during the workshop. It was a little strange living with nuns, but I wasn't there very much. I was too busy dancing. I loved ABT, and I was able to dance some of the biggest roles at the end-of-summer performances. When the workshop was over, ABT offered me a year-round spot to train with them. I wanted to stay, but after everything I'd gone through with my mom, I decided it would be better to go home and finish high school first.

was heartbroken to move away from Cynthia and leave her dance studio behind. For a while, I was angry at my mother, but now I know that she was only doing what she thought was best for me. I moved home and returned to my high school for my junior year. I also began studying ballet with a new teacher, Diane Lauridsen at the Lauridsen Ballet Center. Diane had been a dancer with the American Ballet Theatre, and she was an excellent teacher.

$\mathcal{I}$ came home from San Francisco feeling energized. I set my sights on a summer workshop with the best ballet company in the country: American Ballet Theatre in New York City, also known as ABT. I wanted to spend all of my time dancing. I didn't want to go home to my family on the weekends anymore. But my mother decided that it was time for me to move back home. She was worried that spending all of my time training wasn't healthy. She also felt that Cynthia was coming between us. My mother told me I had to go back to high school and find a new dance teacher.

WELCOME TO THE
SAN FRANCISCO
BALLET SCHOOL

*L*ater that year, I applied for a summer workshop at all of the top ballet schools in the country. There, young dancers come to take classes and perform to see if they have potential to join a ballet company. I was accepted to almost all of them, but I chose to attend the San Francisco Ballet School because it was the closest to home. They offered me a full scholarship, and I spent all summer there training and taking advanced classes. The summer workshop really helped me understand how much I had left to learn. At the end of the summer, the school offered me a spot to train with them year-round. But I wasn't quite ready to leave my family and Cynthia behind, so I said no.

When I was fifteen, Cynthia offered to homeschool me so that I could focus more time on my ballet training. That allowed me to complete my schoolwork in the mornings and spend all afternoon and evening dancing. The next spring, I danced a new version of my Kitri solo from *Don Quixote* at the Los Angeles Music Center Spotlight Awards. I won the first-prize **scholarship** and appeared in the newspaper.

MISTY COPELAND

*C*ynthia had me watch ballet performances in the evenings after my classes, and she gave me amazing books about ballet to read. She even took me to see Paloma Herrera, one of my favorite ballerinas, perform. Cynthia also arranged for me to dance in some live performances. I starred as Clara in *The Nutcracker*, Kitri in *Don Quixote*, and again as Clara in a special all–African American production of *The Nutcracker* renamed *The Chocolate Nutcracker*.

*C*ynthia couldn't bear to see me give up on my dreams. She offered to let me come live with her and her family during the week so I could focus on ballet. My mom was nervous about me living away from my family, but she said yes. So I moved in with Cynthia. I loved it. Her home was much nicer than the place my family had been living in, and her husband was an excellent cook. Mostly, I loved having so much time for ballet.

BALLET 1995

DANCE

EN POINTE 1995

I couldn't get enough of ballet. I watched videos of great ballerinas and carried ballet magazines in my backpack. I spent all of my spare time practicing. But my family was having money problems, even with my mom and older siblings all working. After about a year, my mom decided I needed to quit ballet. She didn't think it was fair for me to spend all of my time dancing when everyone else in the family was working so hard. I was devastated. I wanted to help out at home, but I didn't want to quit ballet.

*B*allet came naturally to me, and I learned very quickly. Cynthia realized I needed to be in more advanced classes. She offered me free lessons at her dance studio, and Elizabeth offered to pay for my supplies, including ballet slippers, **pointe shoes**, **leotards**, and tights. They were both so kind, and it meant a lot that my teachers believed in me.

I was thirteen when I started classes at Cynthia's studio. I quickly realized just how much I had to learn. Most dancers start taking lessons when they are in preschool. They learn the basic steps at the **barre** before moving on to choreographed dances, leaps, and spins. Since I started dancing so late, I had to take beginner's classes with the little kids! I also took classes with the more advanced students. I had to learn everything all at once to catch up. My training was so fast-paced that I danced **en pointe** for the first time after only three months of lessons. It usually takes years of practice before a ballerina does that!

My mom worked long hours. After school each day, my siblings and I would go to the Boys & Girls Club until our mom could pick us up. We would usually hang out, do homework, or play basketball. But Elizabeth suggested I try the ballet class there. I was nervous, but I gave the ballet class a try. I felt awkward and unsure at first, but the teacher, Cynthia Bradley, was very patient. She took extra time to teach me the new steps, and she never made me feel bad when I needed a little extra practice.

My job as captain was to lead **rehearsals** and help our coach choreograph our routines. Our coach was Elizabeth Cantine. She had studied ballet when she was younger, and she taught our team some ballet steps and jumps. I learned quickly, and Elizabeth could see I had a natural talent for ballet. I loved adding ballet steps to our routines.

When I was seven, I saw a movie about Nadia Comaneci, a famous gymnast. I wanted to be just like her. I watched the movie over and over again. I practiced backbends, splits, and cartwheels for hours. My elementary school didn't have a gymnastics team, but later, my middle school had a **drill team**. My sister Erica had been the star of the drill team when she was in middle school, and I knew I could do it, too. I practiced for my audition for days. I made the drill team—and I was named captain!

I was a shy and quiet child. I worked hard in school and got good grades, but I hated when the teacher called on me in class. At home, I always let my louder siblings run the show. So everyone was surprised that I was a natural performer. I entered the elementary school talent show with Erica and Chris when I was five years old. We sang and danced to the song "Please, Mr. Postman." Once I got up on stage, it was like a whole new Misty was born! I loved everything about it—especially the applause. After that, I spent lots of time **choreographing** dances to Mariah Carey songs and imagining myself in front of a crowd.